C IN ACTION: REAL-WORLD PROGRAMMING TECHNIQUES

AKASH RAJAK

Made with ♥ on the Notion Press Platform
www.notionpress.com

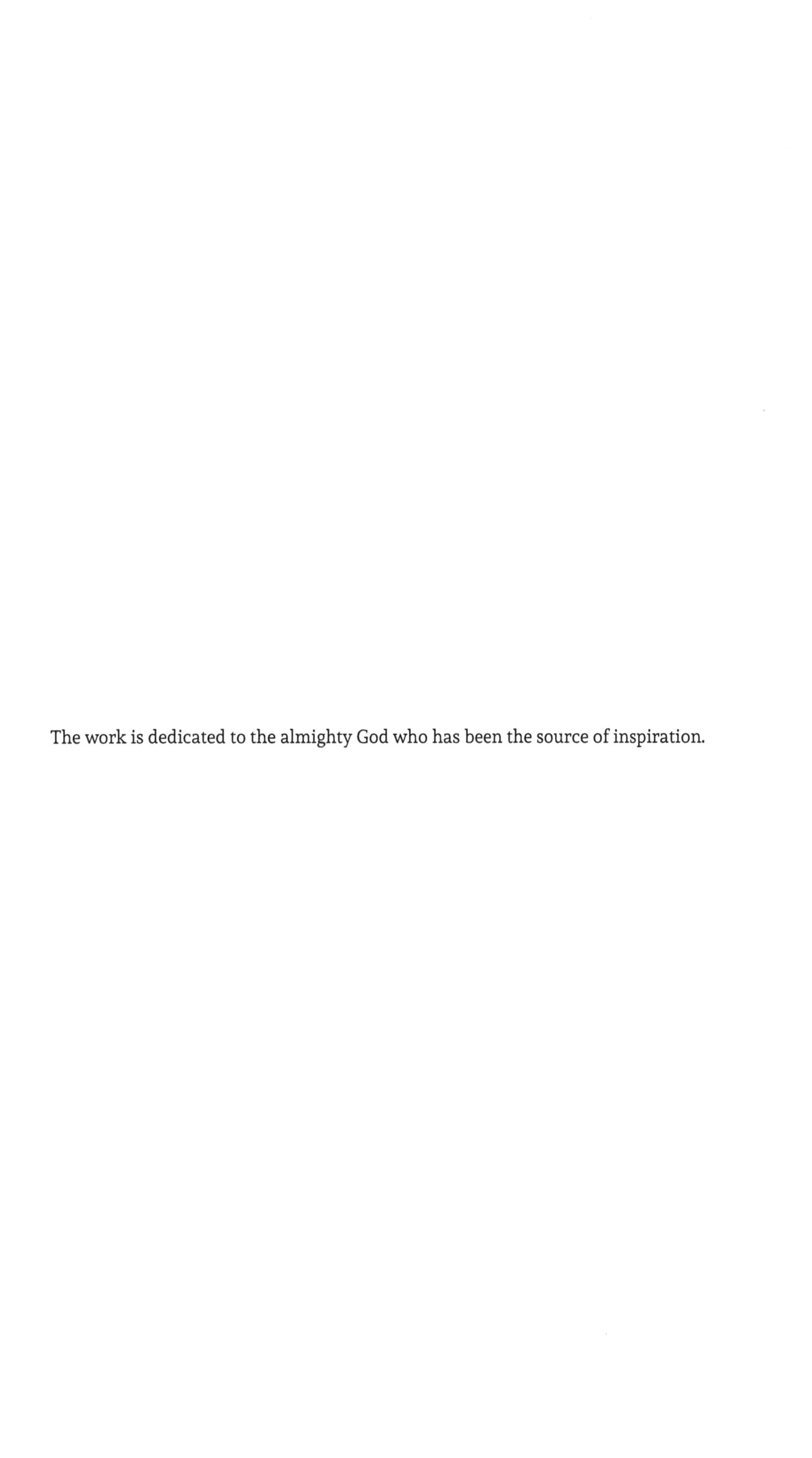

The work is dedicated to the almighty God who has been the source of inspiration.

Contents

Foreword

In the ever-evolving world of software development, the C programming language has maintained its relevance and importance for decades. As one of the foundational languages of modern computing, C provides the building blocks for many other languages and is integral to the development of operating systems, embedded systems, and performance-critical applications. Its power, efficiency, and flexibility have made it a staple in the toolkit of programmers around the globe.

"C in Action: Real-World Programming Techniques" is a testament to the enduring significance of C. This book is not just another introduction to the language; it is a comprehensive guide designed to bridge the gap between theoretical understanding and practical application. Whether you are a seasoned developer looking to refine your skills or a newcomer eager to learn the ropes, this book offers valuable insights and hands-on techniques that will enhance your programming prowess.

The journey you are about to embark on is filled with real-world examples, practical tips, and best practices that have been honed through years of experience. Each chapter is crafted to provide a deep dive into the concepts and applications of C, ensuring that you not only understand the "how" but also the "why" behind each technique. From the basics of syntax and control structures to the complexities of memory management and system programming, this book covers it all.

What sets this book apart is its focus on real-world programming techniques. The examples and exercises are derived from actual scenarios encountered in professional programming, giving you a taste of what it is like to solve problems and build solutions in a real-world context. By the end of this book, you will have the confidence and skills to tackle complex programming challenges and create efficient, reliable, and high-performance applications.

The author's dedication to the craft of programming shines through in every page. With a clear and engaging writing style, the concepts are presented in a way that is accessible and easy to grasp. The step-by-step approach ensures that readers of all levels can follow along and gain a solid understanding of each topic. The inclusion of tips, tricks, and common pitfalls to avoid further enriches the learning experience.

As you delve into the pages of "C in Action: Real-World Programming Techniques," I encourage you to approach each chapter with curiosity and an eagerness to learn. The knowledge and skills you gain here will serve you well in your programming journey, opening doors to new opportunities and enabling you to create impactful software solutions.

Welcome to the world of C programming. Let's get started.

Preface

Welcome to "C in Action: Real-World Programming Techniques." This book is a culmination of years of experience, exploration, and passion for the C programming language. Our goal in writing this book is to provide a comprehensive guide that bridges the gap between theoretical knowledge and practical application, enabling you to leverage the full power of C in your programming endeavors.

C has always been more than just a programming language to me; it has been a tool for crafting solutions, solving problems, and building systems that stand the test of time. Its simplicity and elegance, combined with its powerful capabilities, make it an indispensable language for both beginners and seasoned programmers. Throughout my career, I have witnessed the transformative impact of mastering C, and it is this experience that I wish to share with you through this book.

This book is structured to cater to a wide range of readers, from those taking their first steps in programming to experienced developers looking to refine their skills. Each chapter is designed to introduce and build upon key concepts, providing you with a solid foundation and progressively challenging you with more complex topics. The real-world examples and exercises are crafted to reflect the kinds of problems you will encounter in professional programming, ensuring that you gain practical, applicable skills.

Acknowledgements

Writing a book is a collaborative endeavor that involves the support and contributions of many individuals. We are deeply grateful to those who have supported us throughout the process of creating this book on C programming.

We also extend my gratitude to the editorial team at **Notion Press** for their expertise and commitment to producing a high-quality publication. Their attention to detail and dedication to the project have been instrumental in bringing this book to fruition.

Special thanks to our colleagues and friends in the programming community, who provided insightful comments and suggestions. Their real-world experiences and knowledge have enriched the content and made it more practical and relevant.

To our family and friends, thank you for your patience and understanding during the long hours we spent working on this project. Your support and encouragement were crucial in maintaining my motivation and focus.

Lastly, we would like to acknowledge the countless authors, programmers, and educators whose work laid the foundation for this book. Their contributions to the field of C programming have provided a wealth of knowledge and inspiration.

Thank you all for your support and for making this book possible.

Akash Rajak, Ankit Verma, Amit Kumar &Vidushi

Prologue

In the vast and ever-evolving landscape of programming languages, C stands as a timeless beacon. Born in the early 1970s at Bell Labs, C has since become the cornerstone of modern software development. Its influence permeates countless other languages, and its syntax and concepts are foundational to the coding practices we use today. But what makes C so enduringly significant?

The answer lies in C's unique blend of simplicity and power. It offers a minimalist approach to programming while granting developers fine-grained control over system resources. This duality allows C to be both a high-level language for application development and a low-level tool for system programming. Whether you are writing a complex algorithm, developing an operating system, or creating embedded systems, C provides the tools you need to get the job done efficiently and effectively.

The idea for this book, "C in Action: Real-World Programming Techniques," was born out of a desire to demystify C and make its powerful capabilities accessible to a broader audience. Throughout my career, I have seen many developers struggle with the transition from theoretical knowledge to practical application. This book aims to bridge that gap by offering a comprehensive guide that is rich in real-world examples and actionable insights.

As you turn the pages of this book, you will embark on a journey through the essential aspects of C programming. From the fundamentals of syntax and control structures to the intricacies of memory management and system-level programming, each chapter is designed to build your confidence and competence. But more than just teaching you how to write code, this book aims to instill in you the mindset of a problem-solver. You will learn not only the "how" but also the "why" behind each concept, empowering you to apply your knowledge in creative and effective ways.

The journey of mastering C is both challenging and rewarding. It requires a blend of analytical thinking, attention to detail, and a willingness to explore and experiment. But the rewards are immense. With a solid understanding of C, you will possess a skill set that is highly valued across many industries. You will be able to tackle complex programming challenges, optimize performance, and create robust, high-quality software.

Contents

Chapter 6: File Handling in C

Chapter 7: Dynamic Data Structures

Chapter 8: Memory Management and Dynamic Allocation

Chapter 9: Advanced C Programming Concepts

Introduction

What is C Programming?

C programming is a powerful general-purpose programming language that is widely used for system and application software. Here are some key points about C programming:

Key Features of C

- Low-Level Access: C provides low-level access to memory and allows direct manipulation of hardware, making it ideal for system programming.
- Efficient and Fast: C is known for its performance efficiency, making it suitable for developing high-performance applications.
- Rich Library: The C Standard Library provides numerous built-in functions for common tasks, enhancing the language's capabilities.
- Portability: C code can be compiled on various platforms with minimal changes, making it highly portable.
- Structured Language: C supports structured programming, allowing complex programs to be broken down into simpler modules.

Applications of C

- Operating Systems: Many operating systems, including Unix and Linux, are written in C.
- Embedded Systems: C is commonly used in the development of embedded systems due to its ability to interface directly with hardware.
- Compilers: C is often used to write compilers for other programming languages.
- Game Development: Due to its performance, C is used in game development for game engines and performance-critical parts of games.
- System Software: Utilities, drivers, and other system-level software are frequently developed in C.

Syntax and Structure

- Basic Syntax: C uses a syntax that includes data types, control structures (if-else, loops), functions, and operators.
- Functions: Functions are used to encapsulate reusable blocks of code. The `main()` function is the entry point of a C program.
- Variables and Data Types: C supports various data types, including integers, floating-point numbers, characters, and pointers.

C programming remains a foundational language in computer science and software engineering, valued for its power, efficiency, and flexibility.

History of C

The history of the C programming language is quite fascinating. Here's a brief overview:

Origins

- 1969-1973: C was developed by Dennis Ritchie at Bell Labs.
- Ancestor Languages: Derived from B, which in turn was based on BCPL.

Key Developments

- 1972: The first version of C was created.

- 1978: The first edition of "The C Programming Language" by Brian Kernighan and Dennis Ritchie, often referred to as K&R C, was published.
- 1983: The American National Standards Institute (ANSI) formed a committee to standardize C, resulting in ANSI C (C89).

Evolution

- 1990: ISO/IEC standardized C, known as C90.
- 1999: C99 introduced several new features, including inline functions, variable-length arrays, and new data types.
- 2011: C11 added features like multithreading support, atomic operations, and improved Unicode support.
- 2018: C18 introduced bug fixes and improvements without adding major features.

Impact and Legacy

- C has influenced many later programming languages, such as C++, C, Objective-C, and even non-C languages like Java.
- It remains widely used in system programming, embedded systems, and high-performance applications.

Unix and C

The relationship between Unix and the C programming language is a foundational story in the history of computer science. Here's an overview of their intertwined history and significance:

Origins of Unix

- Early Development: Unix was initially developed in the late 1960s and early 1970s at AT&T's Bell Labs by Ken Thompson, Dennis Ritchie, and others.
- Assembly Language: The first version of Unix was written in assembly language for the PDP7 minicomputer.

Development of C

- Need for a High-level Language: As Unix evolved, the developers recognized the need for a high level language to make the operating system more portable and easier to maintain.
- Creation of C: Dennis Ritchie created the C programming language in the early 1970s, building on the BCPL language and the B language developed by Ken Thompson.

Rewriting Unix in C

- Portability: In 1973, Unix was rewritten in C, which greatly improved its portability. This allowed Unix to be more easily adapted to different hardware architectures.
- Maintenance and Development: Using C made Unix easier to maintain and extend, as the high level constructs of C were more readable and expressive than assembly language.

Impact on Unix

- Wide Adoption: The use of C in Unix contributed to its widespread adoption in academia, research institutions, and eventually in the commercial sector.
- Modularity and Extensibility: C's features, such as structured programming and modular design, aligned well with Unix's philosophy of small, simple, and modular utilities.
- Standardization: The rewriting of Unix in C helped standardize the operating system's interfaces and led to the

development of POSIX standards, which define the interface and behavior of Unitlike systems.

Impact on C

- Popularization: Unix's success helped popularize the C programming language. As Unix spread, so did C, leading to its adoption in a wide range of applications beyond operating systems.
- Foundation for Other Languages: C's design and features influenced many subsequent programming languages, including C++, Objective C, C, and Java.

Legacy

- Unix Philosophy: The Unix philosophy of "do one thing and do it well," along with its modular design, influenced software engineering practices and the development of modern operating systems.
- Influence on Modern OS: Many modern operating systems, including Linux, BSD variants, and even macOS, are either directly derived from or heavily influenced by Unix.
- Continued Use: Both Unix and C continue to be relevant. Unix and Unitlike systems are widely used in servers, supercomputers, and embedded systems, while C remains a key language for system programming and performance critical applications.

Example Code

Here's a simple example of C code that might be used in a Unix environment:

```c
#include <stdio.h>
#include <stdlib.h>
#include <unistd.h>
int main() {
pid_t pid = fork();
if (pid < 0) {
perror("fork failed");
return 1;
} else if (pid == 0) {
// Child process
printf("This is the child process\n");
execl("/bin/ls", "ls", NULL);
perror("execl failed");
exit(1);
} else {
// Parent process
printf("This is the parent process\n");
wait(NULL);
}
return 0;
}
```

In this example:

- `fork()` creates a new process by duplicating the current process.
- `execl()` replaces the current process image with a new process image.
- `wait()` waits for the child process to terminate.

This illustrates how C is used in Unix for process control and system programming.

The synergy between Unix and C has been pivotal in shaping modern computing, influencing a broad range of systems and applications we use today.

Current scenario of the C language:

The C programming language remains relevant and widely used in various domains despite the emergence of many newer programming languages. Here's a look at the current scenario of the C language:

Continued Relevance

- System Programming: C is still the goto language for system programming, including operating systems, kernel development, and device drivers. Operating systems like Linux and many parts of Windows are still written in C.
- Embedded Systems: C is heavily used in embedded systems and microcontroller programming due to its efficiency and low-level hardware access.
- High-performance Applications: Applications requiring high performance and low latency, such as game engines, real-time systems, and scientific computing, often use C.

Standards and Updates

- C18: The latest standard of the C programming language is ISO/IEC 9899:2018, commonly referred to as C18. It mainly includes bug fixes and clarifications to the previous C11 standard.
- Ongoing Development: Work continues on further developing the language, with committees discussing features and enhancements for future versions.

Education and Learning

- Foundation Language: C is widely taught in universities and educational institutions as an introduction to programming and computer science due to its simplicity, efficiency, and closet hardware nature.
- Gateway to Other Languages: Learning C provides a strong foundation for understanding other programming languages, especially those in the C family, like C++, C, and Objective C.

Industry Usage

- Legacy Systems: Many legacy systems and applications are written in C. Maintaining and updating these systems requires ongoing expertise in the language.
- Open Source Projects: A significant number of opensource projects are written in C. This includes major projects like the Linux kernel, Git version control system, and various databases and web servers.
- Interoperability: C is often used for writing libraries and components that can be used in other languages. Its interoperability and foreign function interfaces (FFI) allow C code to be used in conjunction with higher-level languages.

Modern Development Practices

- Tools and IDEs: Modern integrated development environments (IDEs) and tools, such as Visual Studio Code, CLion, and Eclipse, support C programming, making development easier and more efficient.
- Static Analysis and Debugging: Tools for static code analysis (e.g., Coverity, PVSStudio) and debugging (e.g., GDB, LLDB) have improved, helping developers write more reliable and secure C code.

Community and Ecosystem

- Vibrant Community: The C community remains active, with numerous forums, mailing lists, and conferences dedicated to the language.
- Extensive Libraries: A rich set of libraries and frameworks support various domains, from scientific computing (e.g., GSL, BLAS) to networking (e.g., libcurl, OpenSSL).

Challenges and Criticisms

- Safety and Security: C is often criticized for its lack of builtin safety features, leading to common issues like buffer overflows, memory leaks, and undefined behavior. Modern languages like Rust and Go address these issues with more robust safety mechanisms.
- Complexity in Large Projects: Managing large projects in C can be challenging due to its lowlevel nature and lack of modern abstractions. This has led to a preference for higherlevel languages in many applications.

Future Prospects

- Embedded and IoT: With the growth of the Internet of Things (IoT) and embedded systems, C's role is expected to remain strong.
- System and Performance Critical Domains: C will continue to be crucial in domains where performance and direct hardware access are paramount.
- Integration with Modern Languages: As newer languages like Rust gain traction for system programming, C will likely coexist and interoperate with them, leveraging each language's strengths.

In summary, while the landscape of programming languages continues to evolve, C maintains a significant role in modern computing due to its efficiency, portability, and foundational presence in many critical systems and applications.

ONE

CHAPTER 1: BASICS OF C PROGRAMMING

Welcome to the world of C programming! In this chapter, we will lay the foundation for your journey into C by covering the fundamental concepts that every C programmer should know.

1.1 Understanding C Syntax

1.1.1 Basic Structure of a C Program

A C program consists of functions and declarations. Every C program must have a main function, which is the entry point for execution. Here's a simple example of a C program:

include <stdio.h> // Preprocessor directive

int main() { // Main function

printf("Hello, World!\n"); // Print statement

return 0; // Exit status

}

Explanation:

- include <stdio.h>: This is a preprocessor directive that tells the compiler to include the standard inputoutput library.
- int main(): This is the main function where execution begins.
- printf("Hello, World!\n");: This function prints text to the console.
- return 0;: This statement ends the main function and returns an exit status to the operating system.

1.1.2 Keywords and Identifiers

Keywords are reserved words that have special meaning in C. Examples include int, return, if, and while. These cannot be used as identifiers (names for variables, functions, etc.).

Identifiers are names given to various program elements such as variables and functions. They must start with a letter or an underscore and can be followed by letters, digits, or underscores. Identifiers are case sensitive (variable and Variable are different).

1.1.3 Basic Data Types and Variables

In C programming, data types specify the type of data that a variable can hold. C has several basic data types, which can be categorized into primary (or primitive) data types, derived data types, and user-defined data types. Here is a comprehensive overview:

Primary Data Types

1. Integer Types:

- int: Standard integer type.

- short int or short: Short integer type.

- long int or long: Long integer type.

"

- long long int or long long: Extended long integer type.
- unsigned int: Unsigned integer type (non-negative).
- unsigned short int or unsigned short: Unsigned short integer.
- unsigned long int or unsigned long: Unsigned long integer.
- unsigned long long int or unsigned long long: Unsigned extended long integer.
2. Floating-Point Types:
- float: Single-precision floating-point type.
- double: Double-precision floating-point type.
- long double: Extended precision floating-point type.
3. Character Types:
- char: Single-byte character type.
- unsigned char: Unsigned single-byte character.
- signed char: Signed single-byte character.

Derived Data Types

1. Arrays:
- Collection of elements of the same type.
- Example: int arr[10];
2. Pointers:
- Variables that store memory addresses.
- Example: int ptr;
3. Structures:
- Collection of variables of different types under a single name.
- Example:
struct Person {
char name[50];
int age;
float salary;
};
4. Unions:
- Similar to structures, but members share the same memory location.
- Example:
union Data {
int i;
float f;
char str[20];
};
5. Functions:
- Blocks of code that perform a specific task and can return values.
- Example:
int add(int a, int b) {
return a + b;
}

User-Defined Data Types

1. Typedef:
- Used to create an alias name for existing data types.
- Example:
typedef unsigned long int ulint;
ulint num;

2. Enumerations:
- Defines a set of named integer constants.
- Example:

```c
enum Color { RED, GREEN, BLUE };
enum Color c = RED;
#include <stdio.h>
int main() {
int num = 10;
float pi = 3.14;
char letter = 'A';
double big_number = 1.23456789;
printf("Integer: %d\n", num);
printf("Float: %f\n", pi);
printf("Character: %c\n", letter);
printf("Double: %lf\n", big_number);
return 0;
}
```

Declaring Variables:

```c
int age; // Declaration of an integer variable
float salary; // Declaration of a floating-point variable
char grade; // Declaration of a character variable
```

Initializing Variables:

```c
int age = 25; // Declaration with initialization
float salary = 55000.50;
char grade = 'A';
```

1.2 Operators

Operators are symbols that perform operations on variables and values.

1.2.1 Arithmetic Operators

These operators perform basic arithmetic operations:
+ (addition)
- (subtraction)
* (multiplication)
/ (division)
% (modulus, or remainder)
Example:

```c
int sum = 10 + 5; // sum is 15
int remainder = 10 % 3; // remainder is 1
```

1.2.2 Relational Operators

These operators are used to compare two values:
== (equal to)
!= (not equal to)
> (greater than)
< (less than)
>= (greater than or equal to)
<= (less than or equal to)
Example:

```c
int a = 10;
int b = 20;
```

```c
if (a < b) {
printf("a is less than b\n");
}
```

1.2.3 Logical Operators

These operators are used to combine multiple conditions:

&& (logical AND)

|| (logical OR)

! (logical NOT)

Example:

```c
int x = 10;
int y = 20;
if (x < y && y > 15) {
printf("x is less than y and y is greater than 15\n");
}
```

1.2.4 Assignment Operators

These operators are used to assign values to variables:

= (simple assignment)

+= (addition assignment)

= (subtraction assignment)

= (multiplication assignment)

/= (division assignment)

%= (modulus assignment)

Example:

```c
int num = 5;
num += 10; // num is now 15
```

1.3 Control Structures

Control structures allow you to control the flow of execution in your programs.

1.3.1 if Statement

The if statement executes a block of code if a specified condition is true.

```c
int score = 85;
if (score > 60) {
printf("You passed the exam.\n");
}
```

1.3.2 if else Statement

The if else statement allows you to execute one block of code if a condition is true and another block if it is false.

```c
int score = 45;
if (score > 60) {
printf("You passed the exam.\n");
} else {
printf("You failed the exam.\n");
}
```

1.3.3 else if Ladder

The else if ladder is used to check multiple conditions sequentially.

```c
int score = 75;
if (score >= 90) {
printf("Grade A\n");
} else if (score >= 80) {
printf("Grade B\n");
```

```c
} else if (score >= 70) {
printf("Grade C\n");
} else {
printf("Grade D\n");
}
```

1.3.4 switch Statement

The switch statement selects one of many code blocks to be executed.

```c
int day = 3;
switch (day) {
case 1:
printf("Sunday\n");
break;
case 2:
printf("Monday\n");
break;
case 3:
printf("Tuesday\n");
break;
default:
printf("Invalid day\n");
break;
}
```

1.3.5 Loops

Loops allow you to execute a block of code multiple times.

1.3.5.1 for Loop

The for loop is used when the number of iterations is known.

```c
for (int i = 0; i < 5; i++) {
printf("%d\n", i);
}
```

1.3.5.2 while Loop

The while loop is used when the number of iterations is not known and the loop should continue until a condition becomes false.

```c
int i = 0;
while (i < 5) {
printf("%d\n", i);
i++;
}
```

1.3.5.3 do while Loop

The do while loop is similar to the while loop but guarantees at least one execution of the loop body.

```c
int i = 0;
do {
printf("%d\n", i);
i++;
} while (i < 5);
```

1.4 Summary

In this chapter, we covered the basic syntax of C programming, including:

- The structure of a C program

- Keywords and identifiers
- Basic data types and variables
- Operators (arithmetic, relational, logical, assignment)
- Control structures (if, else, switch, loops)

TWO
CHAPTER 2: FUNCTIONS AND MODULAR PROGRAMMING

In this chapter, we will explore functions, a fundamental concept in C programming. Functions help you write modular and reusable code, making programs more organized and manageable.

2.1 Defining Functions

Functions are blocks of code designed to perform a specific task. They allow you to break down a complex program into simpler, more manageable pieces.

2.1.1 Function Declaration

Before using a function, you need to declare it. The declaration tells the compiler about the function's name, return type, and parameters (if any).

Syntax:

```
return_type function_name(parameter_list);
```

Example:

```
int add(int a, int b); // Function declaration
```

2.1.2 Function Definition

The function definition provides the actual body of the function. It contains the code that will be executed when the function is called.

Syntax:

```
return_type function_name(parameter_list) {
// function body
}
```

Example:

```
int add(int a, int b) {
return a + b; // Function body
}
```

2.1.3 Function Call

To use a function, you need to call it from another function, usually main.

Syntax:

```
function_name(arguments);
```

Example:

```
int result = add(5, 10); // Function call
```

2.1.4 Return Types and Parameters

Functions can return a value, or they can be void (meaning they do not return a value). They can also take parameters, which are values passed to the function.

Example:

```
// Function with return type and parameters
```

```
int multiply(int x, int y) {
return x y;
}
// Function with no return type
void printMessage() {
printf("Hello, World!\n");
}
```

2.2 Scope and Lifetime of Variables

Variables in C have a scope (where they can be accessed) and a lifetime (how long they exist).

2.2.1 Local Variables

Local variables are declared inside a function or a block. They are only accessible within that function or block.
Example:

```
void myFunction() {
int localVar = 10; // Local variable
printf("%d\n", localVar);
}
```

2.2.2 Global Variables

Global variables are declared outside all functions and are accessible from any function within the same file.
Example:

```
int globalVar = 20; // Global variable
void display() {
printf("%d\n", globalVar);
}
```

2.2.3 Static Variables

Static variables retain their value between function calls and are initialized only once.
Example:

```
void counter() {
static int count = 0; // Static variable
count++;
printf("Count: %d\n", count);
}
```

2.3 Recursion

Recursion is a technique where a function calls itself. Recursive functions must have a base case to stop the recursion.

2.3.1 Basic Recursive Function

Example:

```
int factorial(int n) {
if (n == 0) {
return 1; // Base case
} else {
return n*factorial(n 1); // Recursive case
}
}
```

2.3.2 Understanding Recursion

Base Case: The condition under which the recursion stops.
Recursive Case: The part of the function that includes the recursive call.
Example Usage:

```
int main() {
```

```
int result = factorial(5);
printf("Factorial of 5 is %d\n", result);
return 0;
}
```

2.4 Header Files and Modular Programming

Header files and modular programming help in organizing and managing large codebases. They allow you to separate function declarations and definitions into different files.

2.4.1 Creating Header Files

Header files contain function declarations, macro definitions, and type definitions. They have a .h extension.

Example (math_utils.h):

```
ifndef MATH_UTILS_H
define MATH_UTILS_H

int add(int a, int b);
int multiply(int x, int y);
endif
```

2.4.2 Including Header Files

You include header files in your source files using the include directive.

Example:

```
include "math_utils.h"
int main() {
int sum = add(5, 10);
int product = multiply(5, 10);
printf("Sum: %d, Product: %d\n", sum, product);
return 0;
}
```

2.4.3 Implementing Functions in Source Files

Define the functions declared in your header files in a corresponding source file.

Example (math_utils.c):

```
include "math_utils.h"
int add(int a, int b) {
return a + b;
}
int multiply(int x, int y) {
return x* y;
}
```

2.4.4 Compiling and Linking

When using multiple source files, you need to compile them together and link them into an executable.

Example Compilation:

```
sh
gcc main.c math_utils.c o my_program
```

2.5 Summary

In this chapter, we explored:

- Functions: How to define, declare, and call functions.
- Scope and Lifetime: The concepts of local, global, and static variables.
- Recursion: Basic recursive functions and their components.
- Header Files and Modular Programming: How to organize code using header files and separate source files.

THREE
CHAPTER 3: ARRAYS AND STRINGS

In this chapter, we will explore arrays and strings, two fundamental data structures in C programming. Arrays and strings are used to store collections of data and manipulate text, respectively.

3.1 Arrays

Arrays are used to store multiple values of the same type in a single variable. They are essential for handling collections of data efficiently.

3.1.1 Declaring Arrays

An array declaration specifies the type of elements and the number of elements it can hold.

Syntax:

type array_name[array_size];

Example:

int numbers[5]; // Declares an array of 5 integers

3.1.2 Initializing Arrays

You can initialize arrays at the time of declaration. The number of elements in the initialization list determines the array size.

Example:

int numbers[5] = {1, 2, 3, 4, 5}; // Initialize with specific values

If the array size is not specified, it is determined by the number of elements in the initialization list:

int numbers[] = {1, 2, 3, 4, 5}; // Array size is 5

3.1.3 Accessing Array Elements

Array elements are accessed using an index. Array indices start at 0.

Example:

int numbers[5] = {1, 2, 3, 4, 5};

printf("%d\n", numbers[2]); // Prints the third element: 3

3.1.4 Multidimensional Arrays

C supports multidimensional arrays, such as twodimensional arrays, which can be thought of as arrays of arrays.

Syntax:

type array_name[rows][columns];

Example:

int matrix[3][4] = {

{1, 2, 3, 4},

{5, 6, 7, 8},

{9, 10, 11, 12}

};

3.1.5 Array Operations

Common operations on arrays include traversing, searching, and sorting.

Example:

```
int numbers[5] = {1, 2, 3, 4, 5};
// Traversing an array
for (int i = 0; i < 5; i++) {
printf("%d ", numbers[i]);
}
printf("\n");
// Searching for a value
int searchValue = 3;
for (int i = 0; i < 5; i++) {
if (numbers[i] == searchValue) {
printf("Value %d found at index %d\n", searchValue, i);
break;
}
}
```

3.2 Strings

Strings in C are arrays of characters terminated by a null character ('\0'). They are used to handle text and manipulate strings.

3.2.1 Declaring and Initializing Strings

Syntax:

```
char string_name[string_size];
```

Example:

```
char greeting[6] = "Hello"; // Includes the null terminator
```

Strings can also be initialized directly:

```
char greeting[] = "Hello"; // Size is determined automatically
```

3.2.2 Accessing and Modifying Strings

You can access individual characters in a string using an index.

Example:

```
char greeting[] = "Hello";
printf("%c\n", greeting[0]); // Prints 'H'
// Modifying a string
greeting[0] = 'h';
printf("%s\n", greeting); // Prints "hello"
```

3.2.3 Common String Functions

C provides several standard library functions to handle strings. These functions are declared in the string.h header file.

Example:

```
include <string.h>
char str1[20] = "Hello";
char str2[20] = "World";
char result[40];
// Concatenate strings
strcat(result, str1); // result = "Hello"
strcat(result, str2); // result = "HelloWorld"
printf("Concatenated string: %s\n", result);
// Find the length of a string
int length = strlen(str1); // length = 5
printf("Length of str1: %d\n", length);
// Compare strings
```

```
int cmp = strcmp(str1, str2); // cmp < 0 because "Hello" < "World"
if (cmp < 0) {
print("str1 is less than str2\n");
}
```

3.2.4 String Input and Output

You can use printf and scanf for string input and output.

Example:

```
char name[50];
printf("Enter your name: ");
scanf("%49s", name); // Reads a string (up to 49 characters)
printf("Hello, %s!\n", name);
```

3.2.5 Common Pitfalls with Strings

Buffer Overflow: Be cautious with buffer sizes when handling strings. Always ensure that there is enough space in the destination buffer.

String Termination: Ensure strings are properly terminated with '\0'.

3.3 Summary

In this chapter, we covered:

- Arrays: How to declare, initialize, access, and manipulate arrays. We also explored multidimensional arrays.
- Strings: How to declare, initialize, and manipulate strings. We discussed common string functions and pitfalls.

FOUR

Chapter 4: Pointers and Memory Management

Pointers and dynamic memory management are advanced topics in C that allow for efficient memory usage and flexible data manipulation. In this chapter, we will explore pointers, dynamic memory allocation, and how to use pointers with functions.

4.1 Introduction to Pointers

Pointers are variables that store the memory address of another variable. They are powerful tools in C programming, enabling dynamic memory management and efficient array handling.

4.1.1 Declaring Pointers

A pointer declaration specifies the type of data it points to.

Syntax:

type pointer_name;

Example:

int ptr; // Pointer to an integer

4.1.2 Initializing Pointers

Pointers should be initialized with the address of a variable or NULL.

Example:

int num = 10;

int ptr = # // Pointer initialization

4.1.3 Dereferencing Pointers

Dereferencing a pointer means accessing the value at the address stored by the pointer.

Example:

int num = 10;

int ptr = #

printf("%d\n", ptr); // Prints the value of num, which is 10

4.1.4 Pointer Arithmetic

Pointers can be incremented or decremented, and arithmetic operations can be performed.

Example:

int arr[3] = {10, 20, 30};

int ptr = arr; // Pointer to the first element of the array

printf("%d\n", (ptr + 1)); // Prints the second element of the array, which is 20

4.2 Dynamic Memory Allocation

Dynamic memory allocation allows you to allocate memory at runtime using functions from the stdlib.h library. This is useful for managing memory efficiently and creating flexible data structures.

4.2.1 malloc Function

The malloc function allocates a specified number of bytes of memory and returns a pointer to the allocated memory.

Syntax:

void malloc(size_t size);

Example:

int arr = (int)malloc(5 sizeof(int)); // Allocate memory for an array of 5 integers

if (arr == NULL) {

printf("Memory allocation failed\n");

}

4.2.2 calloc Function

The calloc function allocates memory for an array of elements, initializing all bytes to zero.

Syntax:

void calloc(size_t num_elements, size_t element_size);

Example:

int arr = (int)calloc(5, sizeof(int)); // Allocate and initialize memory for 5 integers

if (arr == NULL) {

printf("Memory allocation failed\n");

}

4.2.3 realloc Function

The realloc function changes the size of previously allocated memory.

Syntax:

void realloc(void ptr, size_t new_size);

Example:

int arr = (int)realloc(arr, 10 sizeof(int)); // Resize the array to hold 10 integers

if (arr == NULL) {

printf("Memory reallocation failed\n");

}

4.2.4 free Function

The free function deallocates previously allocated memory, returning it to the system.

Syntax:

void free(void ptr);

Example:

free(arr); // Deallocate memory

arr = NULL; // Optional: set pointer to NULL

4.3 Pointers and Functions

Pointers can be used to pass variables by reference to functions, allowing functions to modify the variables' values.

4.3.1 Passing Pointers to Functions

You can pass pointers to functions, which allows the function to modify the variable's value.

Example:

void swap(int a, int b) {

int temp = a;

a = b;

b = temp;

}

int main() {

int x = 5, y = 10;

swap(&x, &y); // Passing addresses of x and y

printf("x = %d, y = %d\n", x, y); // x = 10, y = 5

```
return 0;
}
```

4.3.2 Pointers to Functions

You can declare pointers to functions and use them to call functions dynamically.

Syntax:

```
return_type (function_pointer)(parameter_list);
```

Example:

```
int add(int a, int b) {
return a + b;
}
int main() {
int (func_ptr)(int, int) = add; // Function pointer initialization
printf("Result: %d\n", func_ptr(5, 10)); // Calls the add function via pointer
return 0;
}
```

4.4 Common Pitfalls with Pointers

Uninitialized Pointers: Always initialize pointers before use to avoid undefined behavior.

Memory Leaks: Ensure that every malloc or calloc call has a corresponding free call.

Dangling Pointers: After freeing memory, set the pointer to NULL to avoid referencing freed memory.

4.5 Summary

In this chapter, we covered:

- Pointers: How to declare, initialize, and use pointers. We also explored pointer arithmetic and dereferencing.
- Dynamic Memory Allocation: How to allocate, reallocate, and free memory dynamically using malloc, calloc, realloc, and free.
- Pointers and Functions: Passing pointers to functions and using pointers to functions.

FIVE

Chapter 5: Structures and Unions

Structures and unions are complex data types in C that allow you to group different types of data together. They provide a way to handle related data in a more organized manner. In this chapter, we will delve into how to define and use structures and unions in C programming.

5.1 Structures

Structures in C are used to group variables of different types under a single name. Each variable in a structure is called a member.

5.1.1 Defining Structures

A structure is defined using the struct keyword followed by the structure name and a block of member declarations.

Syntax:

```
struct structure_name {
type member1;
type member2;
// Other members
};
```

Example:

```
struct Person {
char name[50];
int age;
float height;
};
```

5.1.2 Declaring Structure Variables

After defining a structure, you can declare variables of that structure type.

Example:

```
struct Person person1, person2;
```

5.1.3 Accessing Structure Members

Structure members are accessed using the dot (.) operator.

Example:

```
struct Person person1;
strcpy(person1.name, "Alice");
person1.age = 30;
person1.height = 5.5;
printf("Name: %s\n", person1.name);
printf("Age: %d\n", person1.age);
```

printf("Height: %.2f\n", person1.height);

5.1.4 Initializing Structures

You can initialize structure variables at the time of declaration.

Example:

struct Person person1 = {"Bob", 25, 6.0};

5.1.5 Arrays of Structures

You can create an array of structures to store multiple records.

Example:

struct Person people[3] = {

{"Alice", 30, 5.5},

{"Bob", 25, 6.0},

{"Charlie", 35, 5.8}

};

5.1.6 Structures and Functions

Structures can be passed to functions by value or by reference (using pointers).

Example:

void printPerson(struct Person p) {

printf("Name: %s\n", p.name);

printf("Age: %d\n", p.age);

printf("Height: %.2f\n", p.height);

}

int main() {

struct Person person1 = {"Alice", 30, 5.5};

printPerson(person1);

return 0;

}

5.2 Unions

Unios are similar to structures in that they allow grouping of different data types, but they only allocate enough memory to hold the largest member. This means that all members share the same memory location.

5.2.1 Defining Unions

A union is defined using the union keyword followed by the union name and a block of member declarations.

Syntax:

union union_name {

type member1;

type member2;

// Other members

};

Example:

union Data {

int integer;

float floating_point;

char character;

};

5.2.2 Declaring Union Variables

After defining a union, you can declare variables of that union type.

Example:

union Data data;

5.2.3 Accessing Union Members

Union members are accessed using the dot (.) operator, similar to structures.
Example:
union Data data;
data.integer = 10;
printf("Integer: %d\n", data.integer);
data.floating_point = 5.5;
printf("Floating Point: %.2f\n", data.floating_point);
Note: When you assign a value to one member, it will overwrite the value of other members.

5.2.4 Initializing Unions

You can initialize union variables at the time of declaration, but only one member can be initialized.
Example:
union Data data = {10}; // Initializes the integer member

5.2.5 Unions and Functions

Unions can be passed to functions just like structures. You can pass them by value or by reference (using pointers).
Example:
void printData(union Data d) {
printf("Integer: %d\n", d.integer);
printf("Floating Point: %.2f\n", d.floating_point);
printf("Character: %c\n", d.character);
}
int main() {
union Data data;
data.integer = 10;
printData(data);
return 0;
}

5.3 Differences Between Structures and Unions

- Memory Allocation: Structures allocate memory for all members, while unions allocate memory for the largest member.
- Usage: Use structures when you need to store multiple data types simultaneously. Use unions when you need to store one of several data types, but not all at once.

5.4 Summary

In this chapter, we covered:

- Structures: How to define, declare, initialize, and use structures, including arrays of structures and using structures with functions.
- Unions: How to define, declare, initialize, and use unions, including their unique properties compared to structures.
- Differences Between Structures and Unions: Understanding when to use each based on their memory allocation and usage characteristics.

SIX

CHAPTER 6: FILE HANDLING IN C

File handling in C is a crucial aspect of programming that allows you to read from and write to files. This chapter covers the fundamental concepts of file handling, including opening, reading, writing, and closing files.

6.1 Introduction to File Handling

In C, file handling is managed through a set of standard library functions provided in the stdio.h header file. Files can be accessed in various modes, allowing for reading, writing, and appending data.

6.1.1 File Pointers

File handling functions use file pointers to refer to files. A file pointer is a variable of type FILE that points to a file stream.

Example:

FILE file;

6.2 Opening and Closing Files

Files must be opened before they can be accessed. The fopen function is used to open a file, and the fclose function is used to close it.

6.2.1 Opening Files

The fopen function opens a file and returns a file pointer. It requires two arguments: the filename and the mode.

Syntax:

FILE fopen(const char filename, const char mode);

Modes:

- "r": Readonly mode
- "w": Writeonly mode (creates a new file or truncates an existing file)
- "a": Append mode (creates a new file or appends to an existing file)
- "r+": Read and write mode
- "w+": Read and write mode (creates a new file or truncates an existing file)
- "a+": Read and write mode (creates a new file or appends to an existing file)

Example:

FILE file = fopen("example.txt", "w"); // Open file for writing
if (file == NULL) {
printf("Error opening file\n");
}

6.2.2 Closing Files

The fclose function closes an open file, freeing resources associated with it.

Syntax:

int fclose(FILE stream);

Example:

fclose(file); // Close the file

6.3 Reading from Files

To read data from a file, you use functions such as fgetc, fgets, and fread.

6.3.1 Reading Characters

The fgetc function reads a single character from a file.

Syntax:

int fgetc(FILE stream);

Example:

```
FILE file = fopen("example.txt", "r");
if (file != NULL) {
int ch;
while ((ch = fgetc(file)) != EOF) {
putchar(ch); // Print each character to stdout
}
fclose(file);
}
```

6.3.2 Reading Strings

The fgets function reads a line from a file up to a specified number of characters or until a newline is encountered.

Syntax:

char fgets(char str, int num, FILE stream);

Example:

```
char buffer[100];
FILE file = fopen("example.txt", "r");
if (file != NULL) {
while (fgets(buffer, sizeof(buffer), file)) {
printf("%s", buffer); // Print each line
}
fclose(file);
}
```

6.3.3 Reading Binary Data

The fread function reads binary data from a file into a buffer.

Syntax:

size_t fread(void ptr, size_t size, size_t count, FILE stream);

Example:

```
FILE file = fopen("example.bin", "rb");
int buffer[10];
if (file != NULL) {
size_t bytesRead = fread(buffer, sizeof(int), 10, file);
printf("Read %zu integers\n", bytesRead);
fclose(file);
}
```

6.4 Writing to Files

To write data to a file, use functions such as fputc, fputs, and fwrite.

6.4.1 Writing Characters

The fputc function writes a single character to a file.

Syntax:

int fputc(int char, FILE stream);

Example:

```
FILE file = fopen("example.txt", "w");
if (file != NULL) {
fputc('H', file);
fputc('e', file);
fputc('l', file);
fputc('l', file);
fputc('o', file);
fclose(file);
}
```

6.4.2 Writing Strings

The fputs function writes a string to a file.

Syntax:

int fputs(const char str, FILE stream);

Example:

```
FILE file = fopen("example.txt", "w");
if (file != NULL) {
fputs("Hello, World!\n", file);
fclose(file);
}
```

6.4.3 Writing Binary Data

The fwrite function writes binary data from a buffer to a file.

Syntax:

size_t fwrite(const void ptr, size_t size, size_t count, FILE stream);

Example:

```
FILE file = fopen("example.bin", "wb");
int data[5] = {1, 2, 3, 4, 5};
if (file != NULL) {
fwrite(data, sizeof(int), 5, file);
fclose(file);
}
```

6.5 File Positioning

File positioning functions allow you to move the file pointer to different locations within a file.

6.5.1 fseek Function

The fseek function sets the file position to a specific location.

Syntax:

int fseek(FILE stream, long offset, int whence);

Example:

```
FILE file = fopen("example.txt", "r");
if (file != NULL) {
fseek(file, 10, SEEK_SET); // Move to the 10th byte from the beginning
int ch = fgetc(file);
printf("Character at position 10: %c\n", ch);
fclose(file);
}
```

6.5.2 ftell Function

The ftell function returns the current file position.

Syntax:

long ftell(FILE stream);

Example:

```c
FILE file = fopen("example.txt", "r");
if (file != NULL) {
fseek(file, 0, SEEK_END); // Move to the end of the file
long position = ftell(file);
printf("File size: %ld bytes\n", position);
fclose(file);
}
```

6.5.3 rewind Function

The rewind function sets the file position to the beginning of the file.
Syntax:

```c
void rewind(FILE stream);
```

Example:

```c
FILE file = fopen("example.txt", "r");
if (file != NULL) {
rewind(file); // Move to the beginning of the file
int ch = fgetc(file);
printf("First character: %c\n", ch);
fclose(file);
}
```

6.6 Error Handling

It is essential to handle errors in file operations to ensure robustness.

6.6.1 Checking for Errors

You can check for errors using ferror and feof functions.
Example:

```c
FILE file = fopen("example.txt", "r");
if (file != NULL) {
char buffer[100];
if (fgets(buffer, sizeof(buffer), file) == NULL) {
if (feof(file)) {
printf("End of file reached\n");
} else if (ferror(file)) {
printf("Error reading file\n");
}
}
fclose(file);
}
```

6.6.2 Clearing Errors

You can clear file errors using the clearerr function.
Syntax:

```c
void clearerr(FILE stream);
```

Example:

```c
FILE file = fopen("example.txt", "r");
if (file != NULL) {
fgetc(file); // Potential error
if (ferror(file)) {
printf("Error occurred\n");
clearerr(file); // Clear the error
```

```
}
fclose(file);
}
```

6.7 Summary

In this chapter, we covered:

- Opening and Closing Files: How to open files in various modes and close them properly.
- Reading from Files: Techniques for reading characters, strings, and binary data.
- Writing to Files: Methods for writing characters, strings, and binary data.
- File Positioning: How to move and query the file pointer position.
- Error Handling: Techniques for detecting and handling file errors.

SEVEN

CHAPTER 7: DYNAMIC DATA STRUCTURES

Dynamic data structures in C, such as linked lists, stacks, queues, and trees, provide flexibility in memory usage and data management. Unlike static data structures, dynamic data structures can grow and shrink in size during runtime. This chapter covers fundamental dynamic data structures and their implementation in C.

7.1 Linked Lists

A linked list is a linear data structure where elements are stored in nodes, and each node points to the next node in the sequence. Linked lists are useful for scenarios where you need efficient insertion and deletion operations.

7.1.1 Singly Linked List

In a singly linked list, each node contains data and a pointer to the next node.

Node Structure:

```c
struct Node {
int data;
struct Node next;
};
```

Basic Operations:

Creating a Node:

```c
struct Node createNode(int data) {
struct Node newNode = (struct Node )malloc(sizeof(struct Node));
newNode>data = data;
newNode>next = NULL;
return newNode;
}
```

Inserting at the Beginning:

```c
void insertAtHead(struct Node head, int data) {
struct Node newNode = createNode(data);
newNode>next = head;
head = newNode;
}
```

Traversing the List:

```c
void printList(struct Node head) {
struct Node current = head;
while (current != NULL) {
printf("%d > ", current>data);
current = current>next;
}
```

```c
printf("NULL\n");
}
```

Deleting a Node:

```c
void deleteNode(struct Node head, int data) {
struct Node temp = head, prev = NULL;
if (temp != NULL && temp>data == data) {
head = temp>next;
free(temp);
return;
}
while (temp != NULL && temp>data != data) {
prev = temp;
temp = temp>next;
}
if (temp == NULL) return;
prev>next = temp>next;
free(temp);
}
```

7.1.2 Doubly Linked List

A doubly linked list contains nodes with pointers to both the next and previous nodes.

Node Structure:

```c
struct Node {
int data;
struct Node next;
struct Node prev;
};
```

Basic Operations:

Creating a Node:

```c
struct Node createDoublyNode(int data) {
struct Node newNode = (struct Node )malloc(sizeof(struct Node));
newNode>data = data;
newNode>next = NULL;
newNode>prev = NULL;
return newNode;
}
```

Inserting at the Beginning:

```c
void insertAtHead(struct Node head, int data) {
struct Node newNode = createDoublyNode(data);
newNode>next = head;
if (head != NULL) {
(head)>prev = newNode;
}
head = newNode;
}
```

Traversing the List (Forward and Backward):

```c
void printListForward(struct Node head) {
struct Node current = head;
while (current != NULL) {
```

```c
printf("%d <> ", current>data);
current = current>next;
}
printf("NULL\n");
}
void printListBackward(struct Node tail) {
struct Node current = tail;
while (current != NULL) {
printf("%d <> ", current>data);
current = current>prev;
}
printf("NULL\n");
}
```

7.2 Stacks

A stack is a linear data structure that follows the Last In First Out (LIFO) principle. Elements can be added or removed from the top of the stack only.

7.2.1 Stack Implementation Using Linked List

Node Structure:

```c
struct StackNode {
int data;
struct StackNode next;
};
```

Basic Operations:

Pushing onto the Stack:

```c
void push(struct StackNode top, int data) {
struct StackNode newNode = (struct StackNode )malloc(sizeof(struct StackNode));
newNode>data = data;
newNode>next = top;
top = newNode;
}
```

Popping from the Stack:

```c
int pop(struct StackNode top) {
if (top == NULL) return 1; // Stack underflow
struct StackNode temp = top;
int data = temp>data;
top = temp>next;
free(temp);
return data;
}
```

Peeking at the Top Element:

```c
int peek(struct StackNode top) {
if (top == NULL) return 1; // Stack is empty
return top>data;
}
```

7.3 Queues

A queue is a linear data structure that follows the First In First Out (FIFO) principle. Elements are added to the rear and removed from the front of the queue.

7.3.1 Queue Implementation Using Linked List

Node Structure:
```
struct QueueNode {
int data;
struct QueueNode next;
};
```

Basic Operations:

Enqueuing (Adding) to the Queue:
```
void enqueue(struct QueueNode front, struct QueueNode rear, int data) {
struct QueueNode newNode = (struct QueueNode )malloc(sizeof(struct QueueNode));
newNode>data = data;
newNode>next = NULL;
if (rear != NULL) {
(rear)>next = newNode;
}
rear = newNode;
if (front == NULL) {
front = newNode;
}
}
```

Dequeuing (Removing) from the Queue:
```
int dequeue(struct QueueNode front, struct QueueNode rear) {
if (front == NULL) return 1; // Queue underflow
struct QueueNode temp = front;
int data = temp>data;
front = (front)>next;
if (front == NULL) {
rear = NULL;
}
free(temp);
return data;
}
```

Peeking at the Front Element:
```
int peekFront(struct QueueNode front) {
if (front == NULL) return 1; // Queue is empty
return front>data;
}
```

7.4 Trees

A tree is a hierarchical data structure consisting of nodes connected by edges. The most common type is a binary tree, where each node has at most two children.

7.4.1 Binary Tree

In a binary tree, each node has a value and pointers to left and right children.

Node Structure:
```
struct TreeNode {
int data;
struct TreeNode left;
struct TreeNode right;
};
```

Basic Operations:

Creating a Node:

```c
struct TreeNode createTreeNode(int data) {
struct TreeNode newNode = (struct TreeNode )malloc(sizeof(struct TreeNode));
newNode>data = data;
newNode>left = NULL;
newNode>right = NULL;
return newNode;
}
```

Inserting into a Binary Search Tree (BST):

```c
struct TreeNode insert(struct TreeNode root, int data) {
if (root == NULL) return createTreeNode(data);
if (data < root>data) {
root>left = insert(root>left, data);
} else if (data > root>data) {
root>right = insert(root>right, data);
}
return root;
}
Inorder Traversal (Left, Root, Right):
void inorderTraversal(struct TreeNode root) {
if (root != NULL) {
inorderTraversal(root>left);
printf("%d ", root>data);
inorderTraversal(root>right);
}
}
```

7.5 Summary

In this chapter, we covered:

- Linked Lists: Singly and doubly linked lists, including basic operations like insertion, deletion, and traversal.
- Stacks: Implementation using linked lists, including push, pop, and peek operations.
- Queues: Implementation using linked lists, including enqueue, dequeue, and peek operations.
- Trees: Basic binary trees, including node creation, insertion into a binary search tree, and inorder traversal.

EIGHT

CHAPTER 8: MEMORY MANAGEMENT AND DYNAMIC ALLOCATION

Memory management is a fundamental concept in programming, particularly in C, where you have direct control over memory allocation and deallocation. This chapter explores dynamic memory allocation, memory management functions, and related concepts to help you manage memory efficiently in your C programs.

8.1 Introduction to Memory Management

In C, memory management involves allocating and deallocating memory manually. This is crucial for optimizing performance and avoiding memory leaks, which can lead to inefficient use of resources and program crashes.

8.1.1 Memory Areas

Memory in a C program is typically divided into several segments:

- Stack: Used for static memory allocation (local variables, function parameters).
- Heap: Used for dynamic memory allocation (variables allocated with malloc, calloc, etc.).
- Data Segment: Used for global and static variables.
- Text Segment: Contains the executable code of the program.

8.2 Dynamic Memory Allocation

Dynamic memory allocation allows you to allocate memory at runtime. This is done using functions defined in the stdlib.h header file. Dynamic memory management is crucial for handling varying amounts of data and for creating flexible data structures.

8.2.1 Allocation Functions

malloc

The malloc function allocates a block of memory of a specified size and returns a pointer to it.

Syntax:

void malloc(size_t size);

Example:

int arr = (int)malloc(5 sizeof(int)); // Allocates memory for an array of 5 integers

if (arr == NULL) {

printf("Memory allocation failed\n");

}

calloc

The calloc function allocates memory for an array of elements, initializes all bytes to zero, and returns a pointer to it.

Syntax:
void calloc(size_t num, size_t size);
Example:
int arr = (int)calloc(5, sizeof(int)); // Allocates memory for an array of 5 integers and initializes to 0
if (arr == NULL) {
printf("Memory allocation failed\n");
}
realloc
The realloc function resizes a previously allocated block of memory.
Syntax:
void realloc(void ptr, size_t size);
Example:
int arr = (int)malloc(5 sizeof(int)); // Initial allocation
arr = (int)realloc(arr, 10 sizeof(int)); // Resize to hold 10 integers
if (arr == NULL) {
printf("Memory reallocation failed\n");
}
free
The free function deallocates a block of memory previously allocated.
Syntax:
void free(void ptr);
Example:
free(arr); // Deallocate memory

8.3 Handling Memory Allocation Failures

When allocating memory, always check if the allocation was successful. If malloc, calloc, or realloc returns NULL, it indicates a failure.

Example:
int arr = (int)malloc(100 sizeof(int));
if (arr == NULL) {
fprintf(stderr, "Memory allocation failed\n");
exit(1);
}

8.4 Memory Leaks and Debugging

A memory leak occurs when allocated memory is not properly deallocated, leading to wasted memory and potential program instability.

8.4.1 Detecting Memory Leaks

You can use tools like Valgrind to detect memory leaks and analyze memory usage. These tools help identify memory that was allocated but not freed.

Example of using Valgrind:
bash
valgrind leakcheck=full ./your_program

8.4.2 Best Practices

Always free dynamically allocated memory when it is no longer needed.

Avoid using pointers after freeing memory.

Initialize pointers to NULL to avoid dangling pointers.

8.5 Memory Allocation and Data Structures

Dynamic memory allocation is essential for implementing flexible data structures like linked lists, stacks, and queues, as discussed in Chapter 7. By allocating memory as needed, these structures can grow and shrink dynamically.

8.5.1 Linked List Example

In a linked list, memory is allocated for each node dynamically.

Example:

```
struct Node {
int data;
struct Node next;
};
struct Node createNode(int data) {
struct Node newNode = (struct Node )malloc(sizeof(struct Node));
if (newNode == NULL) {
printf("Memory allocation failed\n");
exit(1);
}
newNode>data = data;
newNode>next = NULL;
return newNode;
}
```

8.6 Summary

In this chapter, we covered:

- Dynamic Memory Allocation: Using malloc, calloc, realloc, and free for managing memory dynamically.
- Handling Allocation Failures: Checking for successful allocation and handling failures.
- Memory Leaks and Debugging: Identifying and avoiding memory leaks, and using tools for debugging.
- Memory Management in Data Structures: Applying dynamic memory management to implement flexible data structures.

NINE
Chapter 9: Advanced C Programming Concepts

In this chapter, we explore advanced topics in C programming that go beyond the basics. These concepts include pointers to functions, bitwise operations, file I/O optimizations, and understanding memory layout. Mastery of these topics will deepen your understanding of C and enhance your ability to write efficient and sophisticated programs.

9.1 Pointers to Functions

Pointers to functions allow you to pass functions as arguments, store functions in arrays, and implement callback mechanisms.

9.1.1 Declaring Function Pointers

A function pointer is declared by specifying the function's return type and parameter list, followed by and the pointer name.

Syntax:

returnType (PointerName)(parameterList);

Example:

int (funcPtr)(int, int); // Pointer to a function taking two int parameters and returning an int

9.1.2 Assigning and Using Function Pointers

You can assign a function's address to a function pointer and use it to call the function.

Example:

int add(int a, int b) {

return a + b;

}

int main() {

int (funcPtr)(int, int) = add;

int result = funcPtr(2, 3); // Calls add(2, 3) using the function pointer

printf("Result: %d\n", result);

return 0;

}

9.1.3 Function Pointers as Arguments

Function pointers can be passed as arguments to other functions, allowing for callback mechanisms.

Example:

void applyOperation(int a, int b, int (operation)(int, int)) {

printf("Result: %d\n", operation(a, b));

}

int multiply(int x, int y) {

return x y;

}

```
int main() {
applyOperation(4, 5, multiply); // Passes multiply as a function pointer
return 0;
}
```

9.2 Bitwise Operations

Bitwise operations are used for manipulating individual bits in integer types. They are efficient and useful for tasks such as flag management, lowlevel programming, and optimization.

9.2.1 Bitwise Operators

AND (&): Compares corresponding bits and returns 1 if both bits are 1.

OR (|): Compares corresponding bits and returns 1 if at least one bit is 1.

XOR (^): Compares corresponding bits and returns 1 if only one bit is 1.

NOT (~): Inverts all bits.

Shift Left (<<): Shifts bits to the left, filling with 0.

Shift Right (>>): Shifts bits to the right, filling with the sign bit (for signed types) or 0 (for unsigned types).

Examples:

```
unsigned int x = 5; // Binary: 0000 0101
unsigned int y = 9; // Binary: 0000 1001
printf("x & y = %d\n", x & y); // Binary: 0000 0001 = 1
printf("x | y = %d\n", x | y); // Binary: 0000 1101 = 13
printf("x ^ y = %d\n", x ^ y); // Binary: 0000 1100 = 12
printf("~x = %d\n", ~x); // Binary: 1111 1010 = 6
printf("x << 1 = %d\n", x << 1); // Binary: 0000 1010 = 10
printf("x >> 1 = %d\n", x >> 1); // Binary: 0000 0010 = 2
```

9.2.2 Practical Applications

Setting and Clearing Flags:

```
define FLAG 0x01
unsigned int status = 0;
// Set the flag
status |= FLAG;
// Clear the flag
status &= ~FLAG;
Checking Flags:
if (status & FLAG) {
printf("Flag is set\n");
}
```

9.3 Optimizing File I/O

Efficient file I/O operations can significantly impact program performance. Understanding and optimizing file operations are crucial for handling large amounts of data.

9.3.1 Buffered I/O

Buffered I/O functions, such as fread and fwrite, use internal buffers to reduce the number of I/O operations, improving performance.

Example:

```
FILE file = fopen("largefile.bin", "rb");
if (file != NULL) {
char buffer[1024];
size_t bytesRead;
while ((bytesRead = fread(buffer, 1, sizeof(buffer), file)) > 0) {
// Process data
```

```
}
fclose(file);
}
```

9.3.2 Unbuffered I/O

For certain applications, unbuffered I/O (e.g., using read and write system calls) may be more appropriate, especially for realtime applications.

Example:

```
include <fcntl.h>
include <unistd.h>
int main() {
int fd = open("largefile.bin", O_RDONLY);
if (fd != 1) {
char buffer[1024];
ssize_t bytesRead;
while ((bytesRead = read(fd, buffer, sizeof(buffer))) > 0) {
// Process data
}
close(fd);
}
return 0;
}
```

9.4 Understanding Memory Layout

Understanding how a C program's memory is organized helps in optimizing performance and debugging complex issues.

9.4.1 Stack vs. Heap

Stack: Used for local variables and function calls. Memory is automatically managed but limited in size.

Heap: Used for dynamically allocated memory. Size is limited by available system memory and requires manual management.

9.4.2 Memory Alignment

Memory alignment affects performance. Data should be aligned to the size of the data type for efficient access.

Example:

```
struct AlignedStruct {
char a;
int b;
};
printf("Size of AlignedStruct: %zu\n", sizeof(struct AlignedStruct)); // May include padding for alignment
```

9.5 Summary

In this chapter, we covered:

- Function Pointers: How to use function pointers for callbacks and dynamic function calls.
- Bitwise Operations: Understanding and applying bitwise operators for lowlevel data manipulation.
- Optimizing File I/O: Techniques for efficient file handling using buffered and unbuffered I/O.
- Memory Layout: Insights into memory organization, stack vs. heap, and memory alignment.

TEN

CHAPTER 10: MULTITHREADING AND CONCURRENCY IN C

Multithreading and concurrency are crucial for developing applications that can perform multiple tasks simultaneously. In C, multithreading is achieved through libraries and system calls that allow threads to execute concurrently. This chapter explores multithreading concepts, thread management, and synchronization techniques.

10.1 Introduction to Multithreading

Multithreading allows a program to perform multiple tasks concurrently by creating threads. Each thread operates independently but shares resources with other threads within the same process. This can lead to more efficient execution and better resource utilization.

10.1.1 Threads vs. Processes

Threads: Lightweight units of execution that share the same memory space and resources.

Processes: Separate memory spaces and resources; communication between processes is more complex.

10.1.2 Benefits of Multithreading

Improved Performance: Parallel execution can speed up tasks that are independent and can run concurrently.

Responsiveness: Threads can keep the application responsive by performing background tasks.

Resource Sharing: Threads within the same process can easily share data and resources.

10.2 Creating and Managing Threads

In C, multithreading is commonly handled using the POSIX Threads (pthread) library, which provides a standard interface for thread creation and management.

10.2.1 The pthread Library

The pthread library is available on Unixlike systems and provides functions for creating and managing threads.

Including the pthread Library:

include <pthread.h>

10.2.2 Creating Threads

The pthread_create function creates a new thread.

Syntax:

int pthread_create(pthread_t thread, const pthread_attr_t attr, void (start_routine)(void), void arg);

Example:

void threadFunction(void arg) {

printf("Hello from the thread!\n");

return NULL;

}

int main() {

pthread_t thread;

int result = pthread_create(&thread, NULL, threadFunction, NULL);

if (result != 0) {

```
printf("Error creating thread\n");
return 1;
}
pthread_join(thread, NULL); // Wait for the thread to finish
return 0;
}
```

10.2.3 Joining Threads

The pthread_join function waits for a thread to finish execution.

Example:

```
pthread_join(thread, NULL); // Waits for 'thread' to terminate
```

10.2.4 Detaching Threads

Detached threads run independently and do not require joining. Use pthread_detach to detach a thread.

Example:

```
pthread_detach(thread); // Detaches the thread, making it run independently
```

10.3 Synchronization

Concurrency introduces challenges like race conditions, where multiple threads access shared data simultaneously, leading to inconsistent or incorrect results. Synchronization mechanisms are used to manage access to shared resources and prevent such issues.

10.3.1 Mutexes

A mutex (mutual exclusion) is used to protect shared resources from concurrent access.

Syntax:

```
int pthread_mutex_init(pthread_mutex_t mutex, const pthread_mutexattr_t attr);
int pthread_mutex_lock(pthread_mutex_t mutex);
int pthread_mutex_unlock(pthread_mutex_t mutex);
int pthread_mutex_destroy(pthread_mutex_t mutex);
```

Example:

```
pthread_mutex_t mutex;
void threadFunction(void arg) {
pthread_mutex_lock(&mutex);
// Critical section: access shared resource
pthread_mutex_unlock(&mutex);
return NULL;
}
int main() {
pthread_mutex_init(&mutex, NULL);
pthread_t thread1, thread2;
pthread_create(&thread1, NULL, threadFunction, NULL);
pthread_create(&thread2, NULL, threadFunction, NULL);
pthread_join(thread1, NULL);
pthread_join(thread2, NULL);
pthread_mutex_destroy(&mutex);
return 0;
}
```

10.3.2 Condition Variables

Condition variables are used to synchronize threads based on certain conditions.

Syntax:

```
int pthread_cond_wait(pthread_cond_t cond, pthread_mutex_t mutex);
int pthread_cond_signal(pthread_cond_t cond);
```

```
int pthread_cond_broadcast(pthread_cond_t cond);
int pthread_cond_init(pthread_cond_t cond, const pthread_condattr_t attr);
int pthread_cond_destroy(pthread_cond_t cond);
```

Example:

```
pthread_cond_t cond;
pthread_mutex_t mutex;
void producer(void arg) {
pthread_mutex_lock(&mutex);
// Produce data
pthread_cond_signal(&cond); // Notify consumer
pthread_mutex_unlock(&mutex);
return NULL;
}
void consumer(void arg) {
pthread_mutex_lock(&mutex);
pthread_cond_wait(&cond, &mutex); // Wait for producer
// Consume data
pthread_mutex_unlock(&mutex);
return NULL;
}
int main() {
pthread_cond_init(&cond, NULL);
pthread_mutex_init(&mutex, NULL);
pthread_t prodThread, consThread;
pthread_create(&prodThread, NULL, producer, NULL);
pthread_create(&consThread, NULL, consumer, NULL);
pthread_join(prodThread, NULL);
pthread_join(consThread, NULL);
pthread_cond_destroy(&cond);
pthread_mutex_destroy(&mutex);
return 0;
}
```

10.3.3 Semaphores

Semaphores are used to control access to a common resource by multiple threads.

Including Semaphore Library:

```
include <semaphore.h>
```

Syntax:

```
int sem_init(sem_t sem, int pshared, unsigned int value);
int sem_wait(sem_t sem);
int sem_post(sem_t sem);
int sem_destroy(sem_t sem);
```

Example:

```
sem_t semaphore;
void threadFunction(void arg) {
sem_wait(&semaphore);
// Critical section
sem_post(&semaphore);
return NULL;
```

```
}
int main() {
sem_init(&semaphore, 0, 1);
pthread_t thread1, thread2;
pthread_create(&thread1, NULL, threadFunction, NULL);
pthread_create(&thread2, NULL, threadFunction, NULL);
pthread_join(thread1, NULL);
pthread_join(thread2, NULL);
sem_destroy(&semaphore);
return 0;
}
```

10.4 Avoiding Common Pitfalls

10.4.1 Deadlocks

A deadlock occurs when two or more threads are waiting for each other to release resources, causing all threads to be blocked.

Avoid Deadlocks by:

Acquiring Locks in a Consistent Order: Ensure all threads acquire locks in the same order.

Using Timeout Mechanisms: Implement timeouts to prevent threads from waiting indefinitely.

10.4.2 Race Conditions

Race conditions occur when multiple threads access shared data simultaneously, leading to unpredictable results.

Prevent Race Conditions by:

Using Mutexes and Synchronization Mechanisms: Protect critical sections to ensure only one thread accesses shared data at a time.

10.4.3 Resource Starvation

Resource starvation happens when a thread is perpetually denied access to resources due to other threads constantly acquiring them.

Avoid Starvation by:

Using Fair Synchronization Mechanisms: Ensure fair access to shared resources, such as using condition variables with signaling.

10.5 Summary

In this chapter, we covered:

- Introduction to Multithreading: Understanding threads, benefits, and differences from processes.
- Creating and Managing Threads: Using pthread functions to create, manage, and join threads.
- Synchronization: Mechanisms like mutexes, condition variables, and semaphores to manage concurrent access to resources.
- Avoiding Pitfalls: Strategies to prevent deadlocks, race conditions, and resource starvation.

Appendices

The appendices provide supplementary information to support the main content of the book. They include additional resources, reference materials, and tools for C programming. These sections are designed to enhance your understanding and assist you in applying the concepts learned.

Appendix A: Standard Libraries and Headers

C programs often make use of various standard libraries. Below is a summary of commonly used libraries and their headers:

A.1 Standard Input/Output Library

Header: <stdio.h>

Functions: printf, scanf, fopen, fclose, fread, fwrite, fprintf, fgets, etc.

A.2 Standard Library

Header: <stdlib.h>

Functions: malloc, calloc, realloc, free, exit, atoi, atof, system, etc.

A.3 String Handling Library

Header: <string.h>

Functions: strlen, strcpy, strcat, strcmp, strstr, memcpy, memset, etc.

A.4 Mathematical Library

Header: <math.h>

Functions: sqrt, pow, sin, cos, tan, log, exp, etc.

A.5 Time Library

Header: <time.h>

Functions: time, clock, difftime, localtime, gmtime, strftime, etc.

A.6 Threads Library

Header: <pthread.h>

Functions: pthread_create, pthread_join, pthread_mutex_init, pthread_mutex_lock, pthread_mutex_unlock, pthread_cond_wait, pthread_cond_signal, etc.

Appendix B: Error Handling

Error handling in C is crucial for robust program development. Below are common practices and functions used for error handling.

B.1 Error Codes and errno

The errno variable is set by system calls and library functions to indicate the error type when an operation fails.

Header: <errno.h>

Common Error Codes: ENOMEM, EINVAL, EIO, EACCES, etc.

Example:

include <errno.h>

include <stdio.h>

include <string.h>

int main() {

FILE file = fopen("nonexistent.txt", "r");

if (file == NULL) {

printf("Error opening file: %s\n", strerror(errno));

}

return 0;

}

B.2 perror and strerror

perror: Prints a description for the last error.

strerror: Returns a string describing the error code.

Example:

include <stdio.h>

include <errno.h>

include <string.h>

int main() {

// Example usage of perror

FILE file = fopen("nonexistent.txt", "r");

if (file == NULL) {

perror("Error opening file");

}

// Example usage of strerror

printf("Error: %s\n", strerror(errno));

return 0;

}

Appendix C: C Programming Tools

Here are some tools and utilities that can aid in C programming.

C.1 Compilers

GCC (GNU Compiler Collection): Widely used opensource compiler.

Command: gcc o outputfile sourcefile.c

Clang: A compiler with a focus on performance and diagnostic capabilities.

Command: clang o outputfile sourcefile.c

C.2 Debuggers

GDB (GNU Debugger): A powerful debugger for C and C++.

Command: gdb ./program

LLDB: The debugger used with Clang and LLVM.

Command: lldb ./program

C.3 Profilers

gprof: Performance analysis tool for profiling programs.

Command: gprof ./program gmon.out

Valgrind: A tool for memory debugging and profiling.

Command: valgrind leakcheck=full ./program

C.4 IDEs and Editors

Visual Studio Code: A popular code editor with C/C++ extensions.

Eclipse: An IDE with support for C/C++ development.

CLion: A crossplatform IDE for C/C++ by JetBrains.

Appendix D: Common Coding Standards

Adhering to coding standards helps maintain code readability and consistency. Below are some common coding standards for C programming.

D.1 Naming Conventions

Variables: Use meaningful names; e.g., totalAmount, count.

Functions: Use descriptive names; e.g., calculateSum(), readFile().

Constants: Use uppercase with underscores; e.g., MAX_SIZE, BUFFER_SIZE.

D.2 Code Formatting

Indentation: Use 4 spaces or a tab for indentation.

Braces: Place opening braces on the same line as the statement.

Comments: Use comments to explain complex code; use // for singleline and / / for multiline comments.

Example:

```c
include <stdio.h>
/ Function to calculate the sum of two integers /
int add(int a, int b) {
return a + b;
}
int main() {
int result = add(5, 3);
printf("Result: %d\n", result);
return 0;
}
```

Appendix E: References and Further Reading

E.1 Books

"The C Programming Language" by Brian W. Kernighan and Dennis M. Ritchie

"C Programming: A Modern Approach" by K. N. King

"Expert C Programming: Deep C Secrets" by Peter van der Linden

E.2 Online Resources

GNU C Library Documentation: https://www.gnu.org/software/libc/manual/

C Standard Library Documentation: https://en.cppreference.com/w/c

The Open Group Base Specifications Issue 7: https://pubs.opengroup.org/onlinepubs/9699919799/